MW01135307

THIS BOOK BELONGS TO

I spy with my little eye something beginning with ...

It's an

Angel

I spy with my little eye something beginning with ...

It's a

Decoration

I spy with my little eye something beginning with ...

It's a

Bread

I spy with my little eye something beginning with ...

It's an

Elf

I spy with my little eye

something beginning with ...

F

It's a

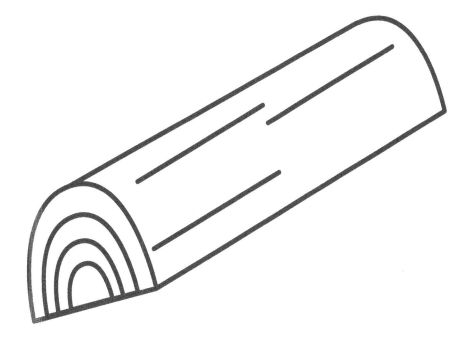

Firewood

I spy with my little eye something beginning with ...

It's a

Pie

I spy with my little eye something beginning with ...

It's a

King

I spy with my little eye something beginning with ...

It's a

Horse

I spy with my little eye something beginning with ...

N

It's a

Nest

I spy with my little eye
something beginning with ...

It's an

Umbrella

I spy with my little eye something beginning with ...

It's a

Vest

I spy with my little eye something beginning with ...

It's a
Yarn

I spy with my little eye something beginning with ...

It's a

Zebra

I spy with my little eye something beginning with ...

It's a

Candy

I spy with my little eye
something beginning with ...

It's a

Mistletoe

I spy with my little eye something beginning with ...

It's an

Ornament

I spy with my little eye something beginning with ...

S

It's

Santa Claus

I spy with my little eye

something beginning with ...

It's an

Imp

I spy with my little eye something beginning with ...

It's a

Reindeer

I spy with my little eye something beginning with ...

It's

Merry Christmas

Xmas

I spy with my little eye
something beginning with ...

It's

Light

I spy with my little eye something beginning with ...

W

I spy with my little eye something beginning with ...

It's a

Tree

I spy with my little eye something beginning with ...

I spy with my little eye something beginning with ...

It's a

Pudding

I spy with my little eye something beginning with ...

Made in the USA
Las Vegas, NV
13 December 2021

37567003R00063